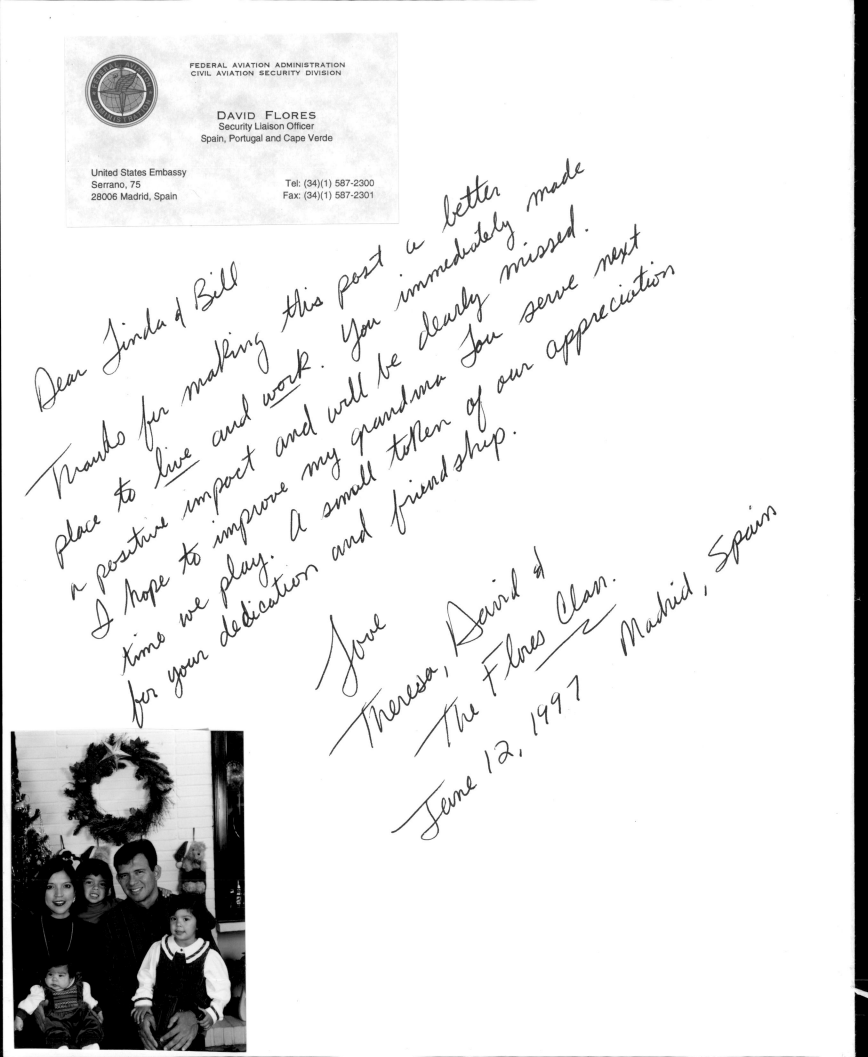

FEDERAL AVIATION ADMINISTRATION
CIVIL AVIATION SECURITY DIVISION

DAVID FLORES
Security Liaison Officer
Spain, Portugal and Cape Verde

United States Embassy
Serrano, 75
28006 Madrid, Spain

Tel: (34)(1) 587-2300
Fax: (34)(1) 587-2301

Dear Linda & Bill

Thanks for making this post a better place to live and work. You immediately made a positive impact and will be dearly missed. I hope to improve my grandma You serve next time we play. A small token of our appreciation for your dedication and friendship.

Love
Theresa, David &
The Flores Clan.
June 12, 1997   Madrid, Spain

SPAIN

TIGER BOOKS INTERNATIONAL

Text
Fabio Bourbon

Design
Patrizia Balocco

Contents

2-3 *Surmounted by the splendid Alhambra, the city of Granada has been declared a national monument because of the importance of its works of art.*

4-5 *The landscapes of La Mancha are embellished by the unmistakable outline of windmills. The castle at Consuegra is surrounded by 13 of them.*

6 *During the celebrated Fiera del Cavallo at Jerez de la Frontera in Andalusia, women show off their most sumptuous and multicolored flamenco costumes.*

7 *Traditions and folklore are the essence of "Romeria del Rocio" in the province of Huelva, the most popular festival in Spain.*

8-9 *Barcelona, the old capital of Catalonia, is along with Madrid one of the two most important cities of Spain.*

10-11 *The Canary Islands archipelago off the western coast of Africa offers charming views and a mild climate year-round.*

12-13 *In the "Romeria" procession, made on a cart or on horseback, participants wear the typical costume of the region.*

14-15 *The traditional costume of Extremadura offers a bold study in black and white.*

This edition published in 1993 by TIGER BOOKS INTERNATIONAL PLC , 26a York Street Twickenham TW1 3LJ, England.

First published by Edizioni White Star. Title of the original edition: Spagna, la tradizione guarda al futuro. © World copyright 1992 by Edizioni White Star. Via Candido Sassone 22/24, 13100 Vercelli, Italy.

ISBN 1-85501-298-7

Reprint in 1996 by Tien Wah Press, Singapore Color separations by Magenta, Lit. Con., Singapore.

Introduction

It is difficult to undertake an objective and meaningful description of modern Spain without falling into clichés and superlatives. It is a modern country of a thousand contrasts, still indissolubly linked to the past.

How can one sum up the sea, mountains, beaches, rivers, futuristic skyscrapers, and silent courtyards in a few superficial comments and statistics? Such a subtle alchemy is impossible. But it is precisely in this play of opposites that we find the greatness of Spain. Lagoons and sweeping panoramas, overhanging rocks and mountain passes, valley gorges and plowed fields, sheltered bays and river sources are always ready to reveal themselves to us in their spectacular magnificence or subtle charm.

Observant travelers will discover windmills and castles, nature reserves and natural parks, gypsy houses, cathedrals, monumental cities, and isolated hamlets on the hot, dusty roads of central Spain. Every landscape, every stone has its story to tell; the very pronunciation of some of the ancient names unwittingly turns into a lesson of art and history. Segovia, Toledo, Córdoba, Valencia, and Zaragoza seem to be waiting for the arrival of the dreamy visitor or the shrewd tourist. Perhaps it is for them that these places have been preserved throughout the centuries.

Travelers will also hear a musical language and absorb even in the most remote villages the heritage of an ancient and proud culture that has endured centuries of counter-reform and decades of dictatorship. Clues to the past can be found in ancient cemeteries, dolmens, prehistoric grottoes, and megalithic settlements which little by little give way to the walls, aqueducts, arenas, and theaters that are remnants of the Roman empire.

The two historical faces of Spain, which have always represented profound contradictions in the very structure of the society, are still noticeable today, despite the significant economic and political changes of recent years. The splendor of churches with gilded altars and the richness of the great palaces, symbols of an omnipotent and boundless power, provide sharp contrast to the dignified poverty of the farmers on the Meseta plateau. There, the centuries-old ways of the most remote interior

regions have not yet caught up with modern customs and attitudes.

Nature, too, provides remarkable contrasts. Given its latitude, Spain should enjoy a uniformly temperate climate with little rainfall. In reality, because of the topography and its distribution, the region presents a vast range of climatic conditions in the course of the seasons. From the sub-tropical environment of the southern zones we pass to the oceanic and windy climate of the Cantabrian Mountains with a great diversity of temperature and rainfall. Central Spain, a vast plateau surrounded by the rugged mountain chains of the Sierras, is characterized by torrid summers and very cold winters.

Along the coasts the tempering influence of the Mediterranean prevails, and here the climate is mild even in the winter months. The Atlantic coasts are characterized by frequent rainfall. Because of the great variety of climate and relief, the flora of the Iberian peninsula is quite diversified. There are a lot of broad-leaved trees typical of high mountains, while grassy steppes and shrublike vegetation cover the regions of the central Meseta, which consists of poor pasture land interspersed with forests of evergreens and cork oaks. The Mediterranean maquis, a dense growth of small shrubs and trees, dominates along the eastern coast and takes on African characteristics in the southern provinces. Where irrigation is possible, sugar cane, bananas, cotton, and bamboo are grown.

Ornamental plants are widely diffused throughout the country, and the magnificent gardens which embellish the cities boast a perennial luxuriance of philodendron, rubber plants, agaves, and magnolias as well as numerous flower species. Andalusia, the most fertile region of the country, has many gardens and plantations, while along the Costa Brava and on the Balearic Islands there is an abundance of umbrella pines, olive trees, prickly pears, vineyards, and citrus groves which are found up to an altitude of 600 meters. Palm groves and the brilliant colors of camellia and Bougainvillea frame the vast expanses of golden beach. The Canary Islands are characterized by their interesting formations of volcanic origin and for their unusual vegetation. A number of plant species found on these islands date back to the Tertiary period and have managed to survive because the effects of the most recent glaciations were much milder in this archipelago than they were on the European mainland.

The fauna of Spain is often referred to as fauna in "transition" between Europe and Africa. In Spain's

16-17 *The Spaniards have many things in common, but there are also many differences between the people of the north and the south, between those of the interior and those who live on the Mediterranean coast. The historical isolationism of the various regions has preserved strong individualistic features which are in turn encouraged by the local administrations. Even the casual tourist can see that the old woman from Burgos, the shepherd from Gerona, and the old Basque gentleman proudly flaunt the distinctive signs of their own ethnic culture.*

18-19 *Using traditional techniques, this old Galician woman repairs a large trawl net used for catching anchovies, sardines, and mackerel.*

16

nine national parks, which cover a total area of 160,000 hectares, it is possible to observe hares, squirrels, partridges, chameleons, wildcats, wood grouse, and even wolves and bears, though these are unfortunately threatened with extinction because of overhunting. On the Rock of Gibraltar (a British possession since 1713 but always claimed by the Spanish government), there are some families of carefully protected Barbary apes, the only colony of apes existing in Europe. The bird life on the Balearic islands, including huge numbers of swifts, Great Tits, and sea gulls, brings flocks of bird-watchers each year. During migrations, large numbers of storks and herons can be observed in the Boquer Valley and in the Tucan ponds. From September to March the salt marshes along the eastern coast of Majorca provide habitat for robins, goldfinches, and rails.

Spain also has an enormous variety of marine life. Its rivers and lakes teem with carp, eels, pike, and trout, while the most common Mediterranean and Atlantic species flourish around her shores. In the waters off the main islands are large numbers of sardines, crayfish, squid, lobster, and octopus, many of which are destined to become the principal ingredients of some tasty local dish. The temperate climate and so much natural abundance have ensured that the region we consider modern-day Spain has been continuously inhabited since the Paleolithic Age.

The Ligurians are considered to have been the first colonizers of the northeastern coastal region, while the Iberians, who perhaps arrived from Africa, settled in the southern regions of the country. The Basques may be of Indo-european stock; they settled in the northwestern part of the peninsula.

Some of the earliest inhabitants left behind paintings of extraordinary beauty and expressive force, rendered with such stylization that mammoth, bison, wild horses, and ritual hunting scenes share some qualities of abstract art. The most famous of these are in the Altamira caves of southern Spain. In the period around 550 B.C. the indigenous ethnic groups intermarried with the Celts to create a new ethnic group known as the Celt-Iberians. The principal colonizing populations of the Mediterranean basin gradually intermingled with them before eventually gaining dominance. In many places, monuments have been left by these colonizing peoples: the Phoenicians at Cádiz, Carthaginians at Ibiza, Greeks at Ampurias. Roman ruins are visible in many places, among the most notable the magnificent theater at Mèrida, the aqueduct at Segovia, and the bridge at Alcantara. In many other places archaeological digs have brought to light the remains of buildings and a large number of objects of everyday use.

The importance of Latin culture in Spain is attested by the fact that the population was already completely Romanized in 71 B.C. and that the poets Seneca and Marziale, as well as emperors Trajan, Hadrian, and Theodosius were of Spanish origin. After the fall of the Roman Empire and the great migrations which brought the Visigoths to the region, the Iberian peninsula experienced a second golden age, both economically and culturally, with the start of Arab domination.

Islamic civilization influenced the western Christian world through Spain. Beginning in 711, the Moors founded a number of Caliphates which soon became famous for their spectacular architecture and for the vivacity of their intellectual life. Andalusia has a number of restored structures that were built in the oriental style. The most important and best-known monument of Moorish art in Spain is the Alhambra in Granada, begun in the first half of the 14th century for Yusuf I on the summit of the hill that dominates the city. From the outside, the building is not strikingly beautiful, but this is characteristic of Arab secular architecture. Inside, there are magnificent courtyards with fountains, water plays, and gardens. Multicolored majolica tiles, wooden coffered ceilings, and stucco work contribute to the exuberant decoration of the rooms. A strong tendency toward symbolic abstraction predominates.

Completely surrounded by walls and towers, the Alhambra consists of a number of structures built over the course of almost three centuries. It had an exceptional strategic position, isolated by deep ravines along the river Darro. Members of the Nasri dynasty chose this site for the most beautiful buildings ever designed in the Spanish-Muslim style. The oldest part, the Alcazaba, is an authentic fortress. There is a Mosque known as Mexuar and palaces like those of the "Comares" and "lions" as well as the Palace of Generalife which was the residence of the Moorish kings of Granada, and innumerable towers and annexes. The entire complex masterfully sums up the the themes of a rich Arab tradition and translates them into exceptional architecture. The load-bearing structures are half-hidden by harmonious finishing touches whose style and elegance elevate them to works of art, despite the fact that the principal building materials used were bricks and plaster.

The builders knew how to use the acoustic effects of water in the courtyards and took advantage of the splendid views offered by the Andalusian

18

panorama. The arabesqued walls, the door and window frames, the gilding of the cupolas, the arches, and columns all intertwine with such equilibrium that they justify the fact that the monument was declared a Heritage of Humanity by Unesco in 1984.

The immense mosque of Córdoba was the largest in western Islam. Built between 785 and 999 in the so-called "caliphate" style, the Mezquita covers an area of more than 23,000 square metres and forms a closed rectangle surrounded by sturdy walls and surmounted by merlons. Inside, there is an enormous patio and a temple which consists of an astounding sequence of 856 columns which, overhung with double horseshoe-shaped arches, form a total of 19 naves. After its reconquest by the Catholics, the mosque was transformed into a cathedral with the addition of gothic and baroque elements. If the Mezquita represents the heart of the old Córdoba, at Seville everything is oriented towards the Giralda, and for this reason has become the symbol of the city. The minaret of the original 12th-century mosque was erected on a pre-existent Roman base, and its austere brick structure rises 93 metres to terminate in a belfry and spire. These were added at a later date when the mosque was knocked down to make way for the gigantic gothic cathedral.

Another pride of Seville is the Alcazar, a complex of buildings which the city's royal family built on the ruins of the palace of the caliphs in "mudejar" style. This is a curious ensemble of moorish and christian elements which takes its name from the so-called "mudejares," the arabs authorized to remain to serve as architects and decorators after the reconquest.

Around the year 1000, the Catholic armies began to descend from the northern regions. After almost five centuries, the Moors finally departed, and a Spanish national state was formed. Although the transformation of the moorish style into a Christian one was rather slow, the beginning of a real Spanish style dates back to the 11th century, when under French and Lombard influence, the Romanesque style asserted itself in the country. The magnificent cathedral of Santiago de Campostela in Galicia was one of the most frequented pilgrimage destinations in Medieval Europe and is the principal architectural work of that period. The extremely solemn interior is dominated by the Capilla Major which contains the tomb of the apostle James. Equally fascinating are the portal to the mouth and the "Portico de la Gloria," one of the biggest and best-preserved works of sculpture of the Romanesque period. The facade of the complex, known as "El Obradoiro," the "golden jewel," was transformed in the 18th century into an excessive and exuberant baroque structure.

As in other countries, Gothic architecture was slow in supplanting the previous style. Indeed, for a long period of time, a number of works, like the old cathedral in Salamanca, were built in a mixed style in which the typical Iberian spirit was able to express itself for the first time. On the other hand, the three famous cathedrals of Burgos, Toledo, and León, built in a later period, reveal a mature acceptance of the French style which had been brought to Spain by foreign master builders. The cathedral of Burgos, an imposing building in white stone crowned by two slender Norman towers, was followed in 1227 by Toledo cathedral with its three sumptuously decorated portals, vast naves, and magnificent stained glass windows.

León cathedral, pride of the whole of Castile, represents the high point of Gothic architecture in Spain; its richly decorated rose window recalls those of Reims and Amiens. The cathedrals of Zaragoza and Seville replaced existing mosques, and the latter, with its immense latin cross-shaped plan, is one of the largest gothic cathedrals in the world. Other eminent examples of cathedrals in 14th-and 15th-century Spain are those of Avila, Valladolid, Astorga, Segovia, and Castile-León, as well as those of Gerona and Barcelona in Catalonia, often overladen with minute decorative features.

A great many of the castles and fortifications which dot the regions of Castile-León and Castile-La Mancha were built in this period, as were many of the windmills which, with their unmistakable outlines, characterize the parched countryside of central Spain. During the 16th century, Spain progressively acquired considerable political importance in the world, thanks to the extraordinary expansion of its dominions in Europe and in its overseas colonies. It became the center of the counter-reformation, with all the consequent religious excesses, and after the death of Phillip II the country slowly lost its hegemony because of the many wars which it undertook in defense of the Catholic faith. Later still, the war of Spanish Succession and the particularly bloody Napoleonic invasion caused huge damage to the nation from both a human and economic point of view.

In the history of Spanish art, Renaissance models were used at first only in a purely decorative fashion in the first half of the 16th century before they were later expressed in a stunning mixture of elaborate

20 *Jerez de la Frontera, world-renowned for its wines, and particularly for its English sherry, is situated in the fertile landscape of the low Andalusian plateau, not far from Cádiz.*

21 *According to Pliny and Strabone, wine-producing was already flourishing in this region when the Romans arrived. Even today, to be authentic, the wine must be made from grapes grown in the territory between Guadalquivir and the sea, then aged in oak casks in the cellars known as "bodegas." The system used for wine production is technically known as "solera," and in the same grape-growing region can yield wine with such different characteristics that they are divided into finos, manzanillas, olorosos, and amontillados according to their characteristics and alcoholic strength.*

ornamentation, late gothic, moorish, and that which was, strictly speaking, the true Renaissance style. It might be said that the Spanish national character was more suited to the grotesque forms of what was known as "Estilo Monstruoso" than to the harmonic and essential lines of Italian Renaissance style. In *Don Quixote,* Cervantes speaks out against the excesses and obsessions of that aberrant style.

Under the strict influence of the counter-reformation, which was opposed to the richness of ornamentation, a style of cold and impressive severity managed to develop. The most representative monument to this style is the gigantic Escorial Palace outside Madrid which was finished in 1584 by Juan Herrera on the orders of Phillip II. Part monastery and part castle, resembling a fortress more than a royal residence, the heart of this immense complex is the basilica dedicated to San Lorenzo, which can be considered the first example of Spanish Baroque architecture. In the Iberian peninsula baroque took the form of a fantastic, animated, often exuberant and uncontrolled style with a tendency for decorative richness sometimes taken to extremes. Baroque sculpture in Spain is limited almost exclusively to religious subjects. The painting of the same period includes some of the most important by European artists. While the genial mannerism of El Greco's visionary paintings confers a great and personal intensity on his religious subjects, the realism of Diego Velázquez produces fascinating portraits of court society marked by an unmistakable critical trait.

During the dominion of the Bourbon kings in the second half of the 18th century, a movement in opposition to baroque began to take shape which adopted the moderate language of Classicism. The first masterpiece to be built following this new tendency was the Palacio Reale in Madrid which was designed by Filippo Juvarra. Later, Ventura Rodriguez designed the Cathedral del Pilar at Zaragoza, while Juan de Villanueva created, with the Prado Museum, the most important example of the Iberian classical movement. The paintings of Francesco Goya, attentive to the cruelty of life, show the effects of the troubled periods in Spanish history.

Civil wars left a deep mark in the history of Spain in the 19th century. These conflicts were caused by the politics of restoration desired by the royal house, by economic backwardness, and failures in foreign policy. Despite the fact that the country remained neutral in the First World War, and there was the possibility of a recovery, internal conflicts became more intense because the most basic social and politi-

21

cal reforms were not carried out.

Faithful mirror of troubled times, Spanish 19th-century architecture is a rather peculiar mixture of styles. One example of this is the Almudena Cathedral in Madrid, which reveals the influence of the most heterogeneous styles. In the same period, Luis Domenech i Montaner and Antonio Gaudi were the unquestioned exponents of a new Catalan style. Gaudi's Temple Expiatiori de la Sagrada Família in Barcelona, begun in 1882, has still not been completed. It is an extraordinary cathedral with daring forms, part neo-gothic and part absolutely bizarre.

Thanks to the substantial indifference of the European democracies, the military insurrection headed by General Franco managed to overthrow the republic in 1939 at the end of a terrible civil war. Parallel to the political and social upheavals, there followed in the first part of our century a profound revolution in the field of art which distanced itself increasingly from imitations of reality. In those years, Pablo Picasso, an exile in Paris, became the most authoritative exponent of this new artistic trend, together with Joan Miró. After the Second World War, the regime of the Caudillo did not succeed in bringing the country out of its political and economic isolation, and only after Franco's death was there a true liberalization of Spanish life and society. Today, the nation is a constitutional monarchy ruled by King Carlos I of the Bourbon dynasty, a sovereign who has favored a profound transformation of all institutions in a democratic sense.

It is thus easy to understand how Spain, regardless of the region or urban center one wishes to consider, makes a favorable impression on its visitors. Every city has something interesting to offer—traces of a long historical and artistic past marked by different and fertile influences but still conserving an original character which makes each one unique. The special character of the towns and cities of Spain is highlighted in a number of feasts and festivals held throughout the year. Among these are the Corpus Christi procession in Seville, the "Fieras" of Andalusia, The Holy Week of Cuenca, the dance of the "Jotilla" in Extremadura, horse jousting and battles between Christians and Moors, races on stilts, processions in costume, Christmas rites, and magical winter celebrations.

Spanish folklore is varied and complex. Many make the mistake of attributing the manners and traditions typical of Andalusia to the entire country. It is evident that the very size of the Iberian peninsula, of which four-fifths is occupied by Spain, has favored

22 *Dedicated to San Lorenzo by King Phillip II, El Escorial was the burial place of his father Charles V and his own summer residence. It was begun in 1562 and finished 21 years later. More like a fortress than a royal palace, the immense construction in gray granite is a parallelepiped with four corner towers. At the center there are bell towers and the enormous cupola of the church of San Lorenzo.*

23 *The grandiose cathedral of Santiago de Campostela, with its magnificent baroque facade, is the best-known pilgrimage destination in Spain and one of the most frequented in the world. Legend has it that the imposing monument was built around the tomb of the apostle James, patron saint of Spain.*

24-25 *In the region of Castile-La Mancha, rendered fertile by irrigation schemes, white farmhouses dot the countryside.*

since remote times the development of completely autonomous and clearly characterized ethnic groups. Though the Strait of Gibraltar has always linked Spain to the African continent, the solid barrier formed by the Pyrenees represented, at least until the final years of the Middle Ages, a clear geographic and historical division from the rest of Europe. Despite the regional traditions, this isolation has meant that a common cultural background has been preserved to the present day.

Religious sentiment, which has been rooted in the popular soul ever since the days of epic struggle to free the land from Moorish infidels, and a persistent memory of a great past have both contributed to the formation of this unitary cultural background. One particularly Spanish form of popular amusement is, of course, the bullfight. No matter how much its popularity has been reduced by other more modern and civil forms of amusement, the bullfight still rallies vast numbers of passionate fans, especially in Andalusia. Organized from Easter to November, bullfights form an almost unfailing background element to the endless series of "fiestas" and "fieras," religious feasts, and commercial fairs in which the sacred and profane are intimately mixed. Alongside the predominant Catholic elements, there are echoes of ancient religions and remote pagan beliefs in the majority of Spanish festivals. These are so numerous and so well attended that one could reasonably claim that no week passes without one being celebrated in one province or the other. This is no small number when one considers that Spain is divided into 17 regions and 50 provinces (47 of these are on the continent and 3 are in the islands). The calendar of popular feasts is thus full of occasions, and the choice is really impressive. Without a doubt, the "Fallas" held at Valencia during the Week of San Jos are among the most important and picturesque of rituals. These reach a high point with the fantasmagorical burning of huge papier-mâché effigies called fallas. Although they are made to look like caricatures of better-known local politicians, they can be traced back to their original function as symbols of human vanity.

The commemorations of the various patron saints are celebrated everywhere with magnificence and considerable organizational commitment. They range from the Fiesta de San Isidro at Madrid to that of San Firmino at Pamplona, during which the celebrated bull race, or "encierro," takes place in the city's streets. The feast of Corpus Domini gives rise to all sorts of folkloristic manifestations in many localities, among which the one at Sitges, near Barcelona, stands out. Here the local flower growers exhibit magnificent pictures made of multicolored flower petals along the streets of the village. Of all the religious events, the one honored with the greatest fervor is Holy Week, in the course of which characteristic processions of penitents and floats reproducing episodes from the Passion can be seen in many Andalusian cities.

The world of advertising has reinforced in our minds the image of a Spanish woman with mantilla and high chignon adorned with flowers and veils, wearing a wide multicolored frilly skirt, while the Iberian male would seem to be forced to wear the plain black suit of the flamenco dancer. While this may be true, to a certain extent, for Andalusia, it should be noted that the female costume in other regions has various styles and colors, generally more sober than one might think. The male costume also differs from region to region. Thus, for example, the dominant color ranges from black in Galicia, Castile, and Extremadura to the red and white found in Catalonia and Navarre. There is a wide variety of hats, as well, from the classic beret of the Básque regions to the gypsy-like knotted kerchief of Aragon and the sugarloaf hats which are worn in the province of Salamanca. In particular, during the sardana, a typical local dance, one can still admire the antique Catalan costume: for the men, red skull caps, doublets and shirts, black knee-length breeches, white socks, and plaited rope shoes; for the women: skirts of varying colors, aprons, and head scarves. As far as dancing, singing, and popular music is concerned, the predominance, at least at an international level, of the most striking Andalusian folk traditions is certain, even though the contribution of other regions is worthy of great interest. Today one seldom sees a person in costume, except on the occasion of some popular feast, and this is a sign of the relentless advance of a technological civilization which is often insensible even to the importance of cultural heritage.

The convergent influences of Byzantine liturgical songs, moorish lullabies, and that particular store of musical knowledge brought by the gypsies who immigrated in quite large numbers into Spain in the 15th century has given rise to a large repertoire of popular tunes of which "fandangos," "seguidillas," "solearas," and "sevillanas" are but some of the more significant examples. Without doubt, the most famous and celebrated dance is the Andalusian flamenco, even though that which is proposed to tourists with this name is nothing more than a rather

tamed down version based on typical rhythms. In the real "tablao," the sound of the "tocadores" (guitar virtuosos), as well as the words and tunes improvised by the singers and the suggestive movements of the dancers, assume a much greater importance. The dance, which is more or less known to everyone, underlines the pressing rhythm with the beat of the castanets and the clicking of heels and expresses mysterious meanings by means of complicated movements of the hands, the fingers, and the wrists.

Like the language, whose rules of pronunciation are different from those of Castilian (spoken in a large part of the country with the exception of Galicia and Catalonia), the popular music of the Basque country is also different from that of the rest of the peninsula. The "auressku" is a sort of turbulent and noisy male war dance, while the "Ezpata dantze" is an even more popular sword dance. Basque sports are also equally original and unusual. As well as the fast game of pelota, many villages have annual and rather exhausting competitions which include the tossing of tree trunks, the lifting of boulders, woodcutting, and bull dragging competitions. In recent years, football has become more popular than the traditional sports, especially in cities like Bilbao, which boast football teams of a certain importance.

Recently, winter sports have become more popular in many regions of Spain, and skiing and other sports are popular in the Pyrenees, the mountains of the Cordillera Cantábrica in the north of the country, the Sierra de Guadarrama near Madrid, and the Sierra Nevada in the south, not far from the Costa del Sol. In all these regions, modern tourist resorts with excellent ski slopes and lifts allow winter sports enthusiasts to enjoy themselves from November to late April. Mountain climbing, both the traditional ascent as well as the more daring free-climbing, has experienced a remarkable boom. For other adventurous spirits, there is no shortage of schools for hang gliding and speleology.

In Spain the distance between mountains and sea is very short. Those who like sunbathing have hundreds of kilometers of welcoming beaches at their disposal. The northern Atlantic coast is hardly ever visited by foreign tourists, even though its beautiful, wild beaches are spectacular. This long coastal strip, interspersed with beaches such as San Sebastián Santander, Villaviciosa, and Pontevedra, begins at the Bay of Biscay and runs along the entire steep and rugged coastline to Capo Finisterre (the westernmost point of the country) before continuing southward as far as the mouth of the river Mino on the border

25

with Portugal. The climate here is not so mild as that on the Mediterranean. Most of the beaches consist of fine sand and are framed by high rocks and steep promontories, while the hinterland is very fertile.

Indeed, the coast of Asturia is known as the "Green Coast." In Galicia the rivers form long funnel-shaped mouths, called "rais," creating particular habitats which are very interesting for naturalists and scuba divers alike. Much farther south, along the Atlantic coast of southern Spain, the Costa de la Luz extends its fine sandy beaches and its impressive pine woods in an arc from Ayamonte to Tarifa, from the mouth of the Guadiana to the straits of Gibraltar. This is the coast of western Andalusia, the shoreline of the sun-blessed provinces of Huelva and Cádiz, which will reward those in search of a favorable climate, beautiful landscape, elegant monuments, and friendly inhabitants.

The Costa de la Luz takes its name from the extremely bright light which highlights its golden dunes and silver tides. The only grayish shades in this dominion of color are the river deltas which divide into a thousand rivulets before reaching the ocean so that land and water merge together in a series of marshes and tidal flats. Along the beaches many relatively new towns have been built. At Cape Trafalgar the landscape becomes more rugged. This was the scene of the legendary battle in which Admiral Nelson lost his life.

Perennially cool winds blow over "Campo di Gibraltar," an area which attracts hoards of young people who engage in competitions on their windsurf boards. The interior offers greener landscapes consisting of more agrarian regions, grazing land for bulls, world famous vineyards, and villages with stark white walls where time seems to pass unhurriedly. The mild, sunny winters here attract millions of birds, and in spring there is an explosion of flowers, feasts, and festivals. The most typical manifestation of Andalusian religious sentiment consists of a "romerias," a several-day-long pilgrimage to a sanctuary which normally turns into a pleasant occasion for meeting people.

During the "fieras" in the villages it is almost impossible to resist the delicacies of the local cuisine. The high point of Andalusian gastronomic expression is doubtless represented by frittura (fried fish), an art whose success depends equally on the quality of the oil and the flour used. The fried food shops of Cadiz are an institution: they are special taverns in which fish can be bought wrapped in paper to be taken away or eaten on the premises. There are

26 *Despite the fact that the Balearic Islands are one of the most frequented tourist areas in the world, the archipelago has managed to preserve much of its natural beauty.*

renowned restaurants but, in reality, the custom here is to wander from bar to bar tasting the "tapas," a variety of appetizers served in small portions and accompanied by the excellent wine of the region. One of the most highly valued is the wine from Jerez de la Frontera, famous since the Middle Ages. The best nectar is aged in oak casks in the cellars of Jerez, Puerto de Santa Maria y Sanlucar de Barrameda in the region of Guadalquivir. Red wines at a strength of 17° are perfect to be drunk as aperitifs or as accompaniments to seafood. One of the world's best sherries is also produced here; only the wines of the Rioja region can compete with those of Jerez.

The rich variety of the valencian cuisine, reflected in the diversities of the region, constitutes one of the pleasant surprises reserved for those who travel along the Mediterranean coasts of the "Azaha." The paella of Valencia has, by rights, been transformed into the most traditional dish of Spain. To wash down a several-course meal or the most rapid snack, a tankard of cool, foaming spanish beer is always welcome. This famous "cerveza" is a particular favorite of those who frequent the red-hot beaches of Catalonia, the best-known in the entire country.

The Costa Dorada, which includes the southern portion of the coast of Catalonia, stretches from the south of the province of Barcelona down to the mouth of the river Ebroit. It is endowed with a series of attractions which have turned it into a tourist area of increasing importance. Situated around the rich and noble city of Tarragona which was founded by the Romans, it extends into an area containing other towns and picturesque tourist resorts. In the interior, the cities of Reus, Valls, and Tortosa merit a visit for their illustrious monuments, as does the walled town of Momblanc.

Along the Costa Dorada a large number of white sandy beaches and small coves are interrupted only by rugged crags of the Garaff. Here, signs of the past and the luminosity of the present-day landscape represent the principal charm of the region. A little farther north, the Costa Brava owes its name of "wild" to the irregular course of the rather jagged coastline, to the luxuriant interior, and to its decidedly irregular panorama. Until the 1950's this splendid rocky coast, which extends from the small town of Port Bou on the French border to the village of Blanes, was almost unknown to international tourism. Little by little it has been discovered and developed to such a point that it is now one of the best-known and most frequented holiday areas in the world. Despite this, the Costa Brava has managed to preserve its natural beauty intact. Alongside the clear water and the groves of umbrella pines, modern towns have been built to blend in harmoniously with traditional, white fishing villages like Begúr and La Escala, famous for its production of salted fish, and Calella and Cadaques, site of Salvador Dali's surrealist villa.

After having been the favorite summer meeting place of the international jet set, the Balearic Islands have now become the preferred destination of increasing numbers of tourists searching for guaranteed sunshine and a tranquil sea. Majorca, Minorca, Formentera, and Ibiza, once refuges for artists and hippies, are justly proud not only of their magnificent beaches, transparent water, and for the mildness of their climate all year-round, but also for the extraordinary liquors which are still produced today by craftsmen who faithfully follow the customs and techniques which have remained almost unchanged in the course of time.

In the picturesque workshops of Palma it is not difficult to come across the famed artificial pearls of Manacor which are used for all sorts of jewelry as well as typical objects made of multicolored glass. Red and blue majolica goods are produced here as well. Spanish craftsmen have a long tradition of working with majolica in several regions of Spain, and now modern pieces are to be found along with those of a more traditional nature.

Excellent leather goods can be found in Catalonia and Córdoba, while wrought iron is produced in both Seville and Toledo. Toledo is famous as well for its production of swords. Albacete is a flourishing center of the steel industry and produces knives and daggers. Copper jugs and dishes come principally from Guadalupe and Granada. Objects woven from esparto grass are produced in the Murcia region. Ceramic products are to be found in most regions of the country but especially in Catalonia, Extremadura, and at Talavera de la Reina, a city which specializes in the production of tiles. Seville is well known for its garment production and for its mantillas. Granada, Almagro, and the Canary Islands are renowned for their open work. The refinement and the originality of Spanish goldsmiths has also been perpetuated to the present day.

Spain has also undergone a rapid industrial development in the past few decades. In the early years of the 1970s there was talk of a Spanish "economic miracle." Rapid improvements were pursued by the government, which implemented policies aimed at maintaining growth levels and full employment.

Barcelona is Spain's principal industrial city, a liv-

ing symbol of Spain's rebirth. It is the exact alter ego of the capital. Free from bureaucracy, studded with a wide range of different quarters and atmospheres, this diverse Catalan metropolis has managed to create a jealously guarded tradition and its own cultural freedom, closely linked to the rest of Europe. Barcelona is a rich and incredibly varied city which knows how to be industrious, bourgeois, and modern while at the same time being Mediterranean.

The futuristic boldness of its most recent constructions are a natural and pleasing complement to its medieval architecture. In fact, the blend of old and new creates a singular harmony. The stunning Art Nouveau architecture of Gaudi could rise as an eclectic symbol of the city. He has left his very personal mark on some buildings which face onto the Ramblas. Today, after having broken out of a period of Franco's neglect which threatened to strangle it, Barcelona is hurrying to carry out the final preparations for the Summer Olympics of 1992. The appointment with this great sporting event is giving further luster to the image of a city known for its tireless professionals and joyful night owls.

Despite its delay in catching up over the years, Madrid does not want to be considered second best. This modern and extremely lively city with dramatic topography and spacious boulevards is the heart of Spain's cultural life. Madrid offers numerous and spectacular art collections, among which the famous Prado Museum stands out. The old city is the most lively part of Madrid, and it is here that the majority of public offices, hotels and the most chic boutiques are to be found. La Gran Via, la Puerta del Sol, la Plaza de Cibeles, and la Calle de Alcala glitter at night with their lights and neon signs.

Madrid is one of the most attractive European cities—her people are optimistic and communicative, amusing and self-confident. New meeting places and discotheques are constantly becoming fashionable. The splendid Parco del Retiro has been transformed into a multicolored stage for rock groups. Young people now also frequent with pleasure the square of Plaza Major which was once monotonous and austere. Every evening, after the "paseo," or evening stroll, the bars become the realm of an active nightlife. More than a simple pastime, it is a way of life. The historic cafes and the flamenco clubs have become sanctuaries of "movida," the new desire for gaiety and freedom from restraint which has transformed the drowsy, provincial capital of bygone years into a dynamic and attractive city that sums up the best qualities of modern Spain.

The Heritage of History

Your country is like mine.
A church, three bars
a castle and a river.
José Tejada

Spain is a country with a very ancient history, and many events throughout its history have left their mark on the character of her people. There have been periods of great glory in which Spain was the conqueror of new worlds and legendary wealth, and dark years in which the country was under the dominion of foreigners who vainly tried to break the spirit of independence and the pride of her people. The pride and the pain of past history remain in the monuments, the works of art, the urban layout of the cities, and the architectural style of palaces, which are all eloquent testimonies of the centuries-old prosperity which characterizes the entire nation. Alongside the works of the past there are also now many modern constructions created by the most fervid minds of our time.

30 top *Ten major roads fan out from Puerta del Sol, the ancient center of the capital. Six of them lead to the borders of the country.*

30 bottom *At the corner of Calle de Alcala and Gran Via is the majestic palace known as "El Fenix," one of the most remarkable buildings in Madrid.*

31 *This aerial view highlights the large fountain which decorates the end of Plaza de Espana and the beginning of the Gran Via, one of Madrid's main thoroughfares.*

The Discreet Charm
of the Capital

The highest capital in Europe, Madrid is situated practically at the geographic center of the Iberian Peninsula on a plateau at the foot of Sierra de Guadarrama. This grandiose city overlooking the Rio Manzanares is a modern and lively metropolis and the center of Spain's cultural life, thanks to its universities, numerous libraries, and its splendid art collections. With more than three million inhabitants, it is the largest city in the country, as well as being the administrative capital, seat of government, and the royal house as well as an active industrial center. The progressive enrichment of the bourgeoisie and the new political course chosen by King Juan Carlos have made Madrid the symbol of the "movida," the desire for liberty and amusement which animates modern-day Spain.

32 top *The Prado Museum, built between 1785 and 1819, is one of the world's largest art galleries.*

32 bottom *Surrounded by traffic-filled "avenidas," the 18th-century royal palace is now only used for the most important ceremonies because King Juan Carlos prefers to live in the more peaceful Zarzuela Palace.*

32-33 *In front of the main post office, a massive fountain known as "Fuente de Cibeles" illustrates the myth of the ancient God of Nature.*

34-35 *Pablo Picasso's famous painting depicting the terror bombing of Guernica is in the Museum of Modern Art.*

The Puerta del Sol, the Gran Vía, the Plaza des Cibeles, and Paseo del Prado are the settings for the life of the city which becomes more intense in the evening when the center of Madrid, bright with lights and neon signs, hosts a heterogeneous crowd which strolls up and down the streets and occupies the sidewalk cafes until late in the evening. The streets around the magnificent Plaza Mayor with their bars, fried food shops, and night clubs famous for their traditional shows are particularly picturesque.

36 top *Young women engage in conversation in a typical bar which looks onto Plaza Mayor. The liberalization of customs has given Spanish women an independence which was inconceivable 20 years ago.*

36 bottom *With its 270 years of uninterrupted activity, Sobrino de Botin is considered to be the oldest restaurant in the world.*

37 *The scenic Plaza Mayor, built in 1619, is still the heart of the Spanish capital and a traditional meeting place for the citizens of Madrid.*

Barcelona, City of Artists

38-39 *Every Sunday morning, on the square in front of the Cathedral of Santa Eulalia, large groups of people form a circle to dance the Sardana.*

39 top *La Plaza Real, once the courtyard of the royal palace, is surrounded by porticoes which are always full of people.*

39 bottom *"Le Ramblas," wide streets which lead to the sea, are flanked by some of the city's most characteristic shops.*

Always considered with a certain suspicion by the people of Madrid, who seem jealous of its boldness and autonomous spirit, Barcelona is a very modern metropolis, an industrial and cultural center which has managed to reconcile jealously guarded traditions and an openness based on its contacts with the rest of Europe. It is Spain's second city and one of the most important ports in the Mediterranean. Barcelona consists of an old center, the Barrio Gotico, surrounded by vast modern city quarters which form the "Ensanche," an area characterized by wide, straight avenues with monumental buildings and industrial complexes. Its historical heritage, its monuments, its mild climate, and the cheerful character of its inhabitants have made the Catalonian capital one of the liveliest, most attractive, and most interesting cities in all of Spain.

40 top From the heights of Tibidabo which dominate Barcelona, one has an excellent panorama of the city. There is a well-known amusement park here, as well as elegant hotels and restaurants.

40 bottom The large port of this Catalan metropolis is one of the most modern and important in the whole of Spain. About 17 million tons of commercial traffic passes through the port in a year.

41 With its multicolored mosaics and fantastic undulated roofs, Casa Battio is one of Gaudi's most fabulous creations.

The unfinished Tempio Espiatorio of the church of the Sagrada Familia, a monumental neo-gothic construction which was begun in 1882, is considered the masterpiece of the creative imagination of Antoni Gaudi. The main thrust of his inspiration is an attempt to integrate into his creation elements borrowed from nature so that the Sagrada Familia seems to have risen spontaneously from the earth in a delirium of composite forms. When it is finished, the cathedral will have three gigantic facades decorated with 12 towers which symbolize the apostles, while the tower above the apse will represent the Madonna. Another four spires, guards of honor to the pinnacle which will represent the Savior, will bear the symbols of the four evangelists. The crypt and the four towers of the right transept have been finished. Construction is proceeding slowly but steadily, thanks to the constant generosity of the faithful.

The Mezquita at Córdoba: A Moorish Masterpiece

The most important monument in Córdoba is the Mezquita, an old Mosque transformed into a cathedral, in which all the originality of the caliphate style comes to light. In the half-light the impressive interior forms a seemingly endless forest of granite and marble columns, whose perspective changes at every step. Above the columns there is a double series of arches which represent an innovative expedient of the builders to increase the height of the building. The octagonal central cupola consists of eight intersecting arches resting on double columns with marble inserts covering the empty spaces, and an ovolo vault is finished with a splendid ornamentation of colorful mosaics.

46-47 *The low whitewashed houses of Córdoba stand out against a stormy sky. After Seville, Córdoba is the most important city in Andalusia. It is situated at the base of the foothills of the Sierra Morena on a plain which slopes gently down towards the river Guadalquivir.*

Seville, City of Art and Culture

Seville, the capital of Andalusia, is situated on a fertile plain on the banks of the Guadalquivir, only 60 kilometers from the sea. It is called the "City of Grace" because of its refined monuments and the gaiety of its traditions and feasts. Fourth largest metropolis in Spain, this cultural center was the cradle for famous painters like Velázquez and Murillo, as well as famous writers. It is also the seat of flourishing industries and an agricultural market.

48 left *The Giralda tower, universal symbol of Seville, was begun as a minaret in 1184 and then transformed into a bell tower for the cathedral. At the top, a rotating statue representing Faith gave the bell tower its present name.*

48 right *At the center of Parco de Maria Luisa, adorned with fountains and monuments, there is the semi-circular "Spain Square" surrounded by the splendid pavilions built for the Iberia-America Exposition in 1929. Here one can admire ceramic panels which represent the allegories of the 50 Spanish provinces.*

49 *The Alcazar of Seville, originally a castle of the Arab kings before being transformed into a royal palace for the Catholic kings, was built in the second half of the 14th century.*

Long narrow streets, rarely penetrated by the sun, wind their way through the most intimate part of Seville. This is the part which still conserves, in the very structure of the houses, the pride inherited from the past. Far from the tourist circuit, a sunny and silent city is revealed to those who approach it with discretion and respect. Protected by high walls, shady gardens open out in front of porticoes which recall Moorish dominion; the splendid ceramic tiles which decorate the oldest courtyards are of Arab origin as well. Today the factories in Seville which still produce such tiles follow the methods of the Renaissance masters, repeating in traditional colors the ornamental motifs introduced by Muslim craftsmen who were brought to Spain to decorate the palaces of the caliphs.

Granada: A Jewel Built of Stone

The famous and ancient Moorish city of Granada is situated at the foot of the Sierra Nevada. Stretching over the countryside of Genil, the city is embraced by the hill which is surmounted by the Alhambra. This magnificent city is considered the very essence of Andalusian poetry, a masterpiece of art and color. While the Arab poet Ibn Zamrak compared it to a lady clasped in the embrace of the river, Federico García Lorca, the city's most famous son, immortalized it with these words: "The color is silver and dark green, and the mountains, kissed by the moon, are of an immense turquoise. The cypresses are awake and they move languidly filling the atmosphere with incense and the wind turns Granada into an organ of which her streets are the pipes. Granada is a dream of sounds and colors."

52 top *The Lion Courtyard is the purest expression of Moorish art inside the Alhambra. Situated in the heart of the royal winter residence, the courtyard is surrounded by 124 columns. At the center there is a fountain decorated with 12 stone lions.*

52 bottom *To the east of the Alhambra is the Torra de las Damas, a fortified construction with vaulted rooms and a small mosque overlooking a vast pool. The whole is surrounded by a luxuriant garden.*

53 *In the southern part of the Lion Courtyard there is the Abenceragi Room, which takes its name from a noble family. The vault is very unusual, with stalagtites overhanging a dodecagonal fountain placed at the center of the room.*

The Wealth of the Centuries

54 *The ancient Castilian city of Avila is situated on the crest of a steep hill at the center of the bleak plain of the Rio Adaja. Its Roman walls, which enclose the old city, are reinforced by many towers which have been preserved intact, making Avila one of the most interesting Spanish cities.*

54-55 *Nuestra Senora del Pila is Zaragoza's second cathedral. Situated on the banks of the Ebro, it was begun in 1681 but was never completed. The large rectangular construction includes a large central cupola and ten smaller ones, while four bell towers rise up at the corners.*

56-57 *The Alcazar at Segovia was completed in the 12th century and enlarged at a later date. It constitutes the most perfect and best-conserved example of a fortified castle in Old Castile.*

58-59 *The Alcazar is situated on the site of a former Roman fortification, dominating the city of Toledo. The capital of New Castile, still surrounded by Moorish-gothic walls, was founded on a granite rise and is surrounded on three sides by the river Tagus.*

People of Strong Temperament

In our very blood there is the
source which has germinated
reason and dreams in you.
García Lorca

Festivals play a rather important role in the popular culture of the Iberian peninsula, where folklore and traditions are kept alive in a completely spontaneous manner. As well as the traditional religious festivals, almost every city and village celebrates annually their particular feast days with feasts, bullfights, processions, musical shows, and games. During a journey through Spain, one could reach a different place every day which is celebrating a local festival, and find all the shops and offices closed. It is no wonder then that the tourist offices publish a very detailed calendar with all the feasts in the country.

60-61 The complex multiplicity of Spanish culture can also be seen in popular events in which the elements of the different regions emerge more spontaneously. Whether they are religious or lay, the festivals are always characterized by the enthusiastic participation of the people.

Blood and the Arena

Universally considered the Spanish spectacle par excellence, the Corrida de Toros continues to attract enormous crowds to the country's more than three hundred arenas, despite the increasing large number of dissenting voices. The origins of such fights are lost in the mists of time, but the bullfight as it exists today dates back to some time around the 14th century. Although the character who most fascinates the public is the "matador" who is carried in triumph or booed according to the audacity he shows, other intrepid men, the banderilleros and picadores, face up to the animal in a precise sequence with the purpose of irritating and draining the strength of the bull before the final assault. The bulls, which normally come from Andalusian breeding farms, can also have their moment of glory if they reveal themselves to be valiant fighters. In such cases the fatally wounded animal is dragged around the arena to do a lap of honor.

Festivals:
Between the Sacred
and the Profane

64-65 At Pamplona, during the celebrations in honor of San Firmino, "Encierros" take place. These are spectacular events in which young people are chased along the streets by fighting bulls.

65 and 66-67 The participants in the bull race traditionally wear scarves and red berets.

68-69 Dressed as penitents, the members of the religious confraternities of Cartagena head for the church during Holy Week celebrations.

Pilgrimage to El Rocio

One of the most typical manifestations of religious sentiment in which the Spaniards participate are the so-called "romerias" which are long pilgrimages to some sanctuary during which the faith supplies the pretext for spending some days in cheerful company.

The most famous "romeria" in the country is that which takes place in the week preceding Pentecost in the small village of El Rocio

in the province of Huelva. This village is practically deserted during the rest of the year, but up to 100,000 pilgrims, many of whom are gypsies, come to pray in a sanctuary where a statue of the Virgin Mary known as Nostra Signora de la Rugiada (Our Lady of the Dew) is venerated. The culminating moment of the Romeria del Rocio is an open-air mass which is followed by the blessing of the Virgin and celebrations with dancing and banquets.

The Colours of the "Feira"

Every year, generally from the 18th to the 23rd of April, the celebrated "Fiera" takes place in Seville. It is one of Spain's most fascinating feasts in which there is a mixture of all the components of the lively Andalusian folk culture: bullfights, flamenco dancing, "sevillanas," and processions in costume. The origin of this lively event dates back to

1846, the year in which Queen Isabella II granted Seville the privilege of celebrating a fair. In the zone known as Real de la Fiera, "casetas" are erected under thousands of colored bulbs and lanterns. Here the flamenco is danced and one meets friends after the morning horse parade in which the horse riders in traditional costumes show their skills and transport ladies dressed for the feast.

74-75 *Andalusian noblemen still practice the "haute ecole" of horsemanship. Their weekly shows are very popular.*

The Sea: Eternal Source of Life

A good part of Spain's wealth has been linked since time immemorial to the exploitation of the country's marine resources. Today, fishing is one of the main occupations in the coastal regions, while the ports of Barcelona, Bilbao, Valencia, and Cádiz are constantly increasing their volume of trade. One of the main factors which has helped the economic expansion of the country has been the growth of tourism, which is particularly due to the beauty of the coastline and a constantly blue sea. The localities on the Mediterranean, the Balearic Islands, and the Canaries are the ones most visited by tourists. In order to remain attractive to tourists, the country is now involved in a vast campaign to help preserve its natural beauty.

76-77 Even today off the coast of Cádiz, the cruel ritual of the tuna fish slaughter takes place following a tradition which has been unchanged for centuries. After having captured a large number of tuna in the narrow stretch of water surrounded by rowboats, the Andalusian fishermen stun their prey and haul them aboard with long hooks, while all around the sea takes on a reddish hue.

77 top Tossa del Mar is a small village in a charming cove on the Costa Brava. Today it is one of the busiest holiday resorts, and it can boast the Roman ruins and medieval walls which still surround the old part of the town.

77 bottom Cala d'Hort is one of the most evocative corners on the beautiful island of Ibiza. The island has a charming climate, and its principle attractions are to be found in its blue skies and sea.

78-79 A group of women repair fishing nets on a lawn in Orio, a fishing village in the Basque provinces.

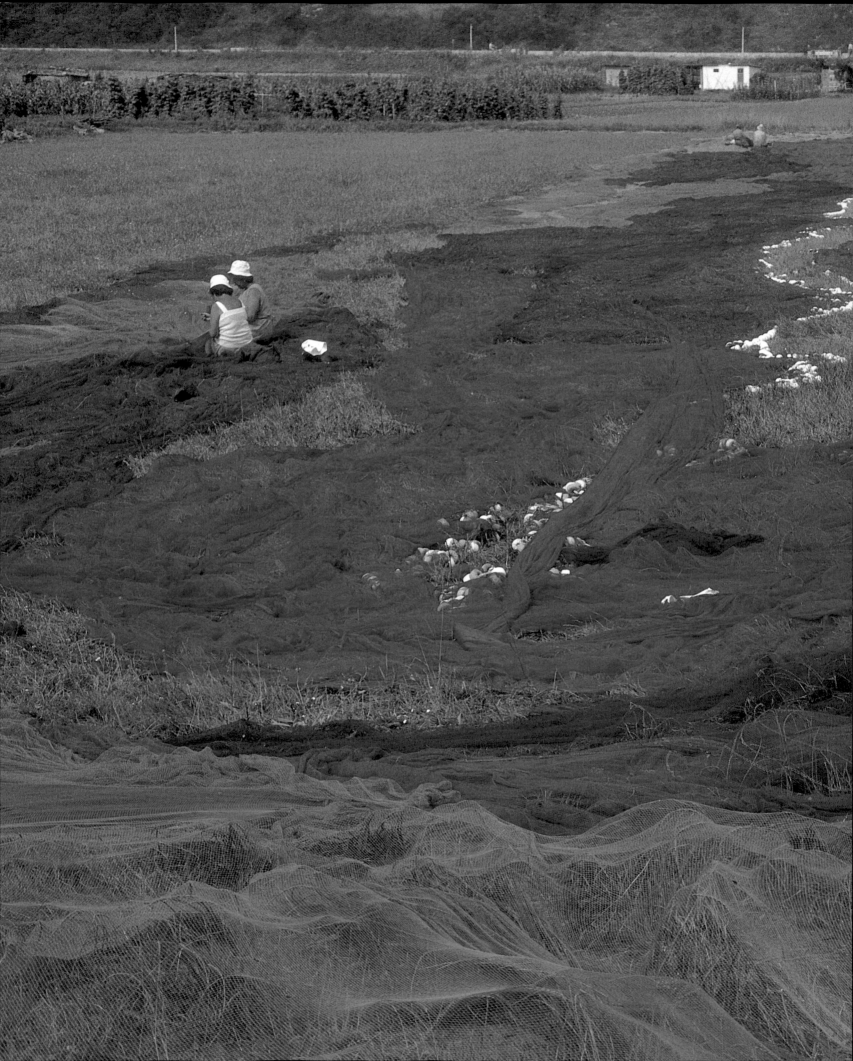

A Miserly Land

80-81 *Near Valdelavia, a village in Castile-León, a couple of farmers plough a grassy slope. With the abandonment of such rural activities, the countryside has lost a lot of inhabitants in recent years, many of whom have moved to Madrid.*

81 top *Agricultural laborers and shepherds live in great poverty, especially in the interior regions where there are still a lot of very large estates.*

81 bottom *These young farmers still wear the traditional dark costumes of the countryside of New Castile.*

82-83 *The most developed sectors of Spanish agriculture are those involved in the production of fruit and vegetables.*

The Grape Harvest

The fertile valley of the Ebro extends across northern Spain, and in the eastern part there is the wine-growing region of La Rioja. This region borders on the Basque provinces and extends to the Atlantic between the Pyrenees and the Cantabrian Mountains. Here, as in nearby Galicia, the fields are always green and luxuriant due to the temperate climate. Harvests are abundant and the grapes are used to produce an excellent red wine which is aged in oak casks. The freshly picked grapes are transported by mule or on the farmer's back, and taken to the old cellars where they are pressed using traditional hand-operated equipment. The grape must is collected in vats for natural fermentation. In La Mancha, another wine-producing region, the grape harvest is an important event closely linked to ancient and deep-rooted agricultural traditions.

86-87 A row of windmills appears to stand guard over this small village in La Mancha. Introduced from Holland in the 16th century, the windmills were used to grind corn. Now they have fallen into disuse, and many of them are in ruins.

Ancient Horse Trials

Every year on the 23rd and 24th of June, the feast of San Juan is celebrated near Ciudadela, the old regional capital on the western coast of the island of Minorca. For a number of days the island's horsemen participate in riding competitions in the streets of the town. The participants wear historic costumes which represent the various social classes and thus keep alive a tradition which originated in the Middle Ages. The heritage of folklore in Spain is particularly rich and varied, tied to historical events in the various regions, modified in the course of the centuries, and experienced by generation after generation with unchanged enthusiasm.

90-91 *The mild, humid climate of Galicia favors cattle breeding, and the beauty of the horses of Pontevedra is world-renowned.*

The Charm of Everyday Life

The quarters of old Seville sum up all the charm of the Andalusian way of life. At Santa Cruz, the white houses open their windows onto the river; the "calles" of San Bernardo bring to mind the corrida; while in the quarters of San Lorenzo and San Vincente the upper-class houses surround 19th-century courtyards. The beauty of these vistas was chosen as the backdrop for some of the world's most famous operas including Mozart's "Don Giovanni" and "Marriage of Figaro" and Bizet's "Carmen." Various city streets claim that Rossini's barber had his shop there.

92 top left *Plaza del Salvador is one of the most popular meeting places in the city and is always animated by* crowds who visit the cafes and clubs of this pleasant pedestrian zone.

92 bottom left *The Torre de Oro is situated on the banks of the Guadalquivir. Originally it was a Moorish defensive construction; it now houses the Naval Museum. It was from here that Magellan set sail on the first circumnavigation of the world in 1519.*

92 right *The "Confiteria La Campana" is one of the oldest and best-known shops in the center of Seville.*

93 *In the Macarena quarter, one of the most popular in the Andalusian capital, a flea market is held every Thursday which attracts many visitors and a number of original characters.*

San Sebastián:
Sandy Half-moon

Aristocratic city on the Basque coast, San Sebastián consists of a historical center surrounded by fortifications which were erected in the 16th century by Vespasiano Gonzaga and by vast modern quarters characterized by long regular Avenidas and mansions built in the French style. Known in the local dialect as Donistia, the capital of the province of Giupuzcoa extends along the sea front and beaches of a luminous cove of the Bay of Biscay. In the second half of September, San Sebastián is host to the International Festival of Cinema.

94-95 *"La Concha" is the principal beach of San Sebastián, an elegant and cosmopolitan bathing resort. Known for its fine golden sand, it is one of the most renowned beaches in Spain. Separated by the small rocky promontory of Pico del Loro, the adjacent beach of Ondaratta is well equipped and always very busy.*

Ibiza: The Enchanted Isle

Lively and effervescent, the capital of the island with the same name is better known as "la Cuidad," the city. Built on the side of a steep hill which rises rapidly from the waters of the Mediterranean, Ibiza boasts a rare charm. Its fortunate geographic position, the blinding whiteness of its the white-washed dwellings, and its slightly oriental aspect make this one of the best-loved tourist centers in the world.

Land of Contrasts

Eternal corner
The land and the sky
Bisected by the wind
Immense corner
The straight path
—*García Lorca*

The uneven terrain of most of the Iberian Peninsula has always hindered communications and made contact quite difficult so that for centuries the country has been divided into isolated regions. Indeed, until not too long ago, the sovereign was known as "King of all the Spains." From the jagged coast of the Canaries to the wavy hinterland of Andalusia, to the steep rock faces of the Pyrenees and the arid desolation of the central Meseta, Spain is a land of singular beauty and strong contrasts in which each of the 50 provinces flaunts a strong individuality.

98 top *The waves of the Atlantic Ocean have modeled the volcanic coastline of the Island of Lanzarote in the Canary Archipelago into bizarre shapes.*

98 bottom *A rural village in the hinterland of Granada is perched with its terraces on the first foothills of the Sierra Nevada.*

99 *The imposing outline of Monte Perdido threateningly hangs over the course of the River Araza in the National Park of the Valley of Ordesa, established in the Aragonese Pyrenees in 1918. The park gives shelter to Ibex and chamois, as well as a fair number of golden eagles.*

Spain's Mountain Wilderness

100 *The National Park of Aigues Tortes in the Catalan Sierra de los Encantos has all the typical characteristics of glacial zones. The mountain chains and the moraines which descend towards the plain create valleys inhabited by boar, ermine, and chamois.*

101 *The Pico del Castillo and the curious towers known as Las Retuertas constitute one of the most singular formations of the Cantabrian Cordillera, which extends parallel to* the Atlantic coast for more than 500 kilometers.

102-103 *One of the last snowfalls of winter has whitened the enormous mass of Monte Perdido and the underlying Valley de Pineta. The Pyrenees, which separate Spain from France, have contributed in keeping the Iberian Peninsula isolated from the rest of Europe in the course of the centuries.*

104-105 *Under a dark and stormy sky, thousands of olive trees grow in regular lines in the undulating landscape of the Andalusian province of Juan.*

Memories
of an Ancient
World

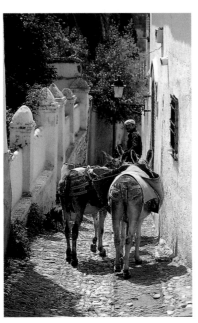

*Under a dark and stormy sky,
thousands of olive trees grow in
regualar lines in the undulating
landscape of Andalusia. With its
sunny and slightly mysterious cities,
its blindingly white walls and dark
entrance halls smelling of
magnolia, Andalusia is Spain for
many people. It might seem a
slightly limiting judgment but it is
certainly not rash because
Andalusia and the Alhambra of
Granada, the Alcazar of Seville,
the mosque and Moorish forts,
Carmen, dark-eyed gypsies,
sun-baked villages and the
chattering of the chicades, bullfights
and processions, sangria and the
beaches of Costa del Sol, constitute
an exotic and enchanted world,
half way between Africa and the
Orient.*

The name Andalusia comes from the Arab "Al-Andalus," the land of the west, as it was called by the Moors who dominated it for more than 800 years. An unequaled variety of landscapes with strong contrasts gives life to this region which was the foremost cultural and economic center of the whole peninsula. The lanes, narrow windows, and wrought iron railings in the Arab quarter of Almaylin, and the immaculate little houses below the Montefrio fortress constitute the historical and cultural inheritance which recalls in a thousand particulars the houses of the ancient Arab ancestors.

108-109 *The architectural elements of few other western European nations can be identified as easily as those of Spain. The steep streets of Andalusian villages, the white-washed houses with rows of chili peppers hanging up to dry in the sun, walls of courtyards adorned with vases of flowers, are all elements which are unmistakably Iberian, symbols of a tradition and a historical continuity which has its roots in the most ancient Mediterranean civilization.*

110-111 *The patio of this patrician house in the center of Córdoba is enhanced by a myriad geraniums.*

112-113 *The countryside of Andalusia has the most varied range of landscapes. In the western zone of the Guadalquivir basin, the province is characterized by a series of hills dotted with white farmhouses.*

Doñana: A Miracle of Nature

In the province of Huelva on the swampy delta of the river Guadalquivir is the national park of Doñana, the largest and most interesting in the whole of Spain. It covers an area of 76,000 hectares and is one of the major animal reserves on the continent. The richness of this area is due to its good climate, its location, its marshes, shifting sand dunes, and abundant fauna. As well as being the reproduction site for an innumerable number of species of fish, reptiles, amphibians, birds, and reptiles, it is also an obligatory stopover for about one million migratory birds.

116-117 *An enormous flock of flamingos flies over ponds in Doñana. In the reserve there are enormous colonies of birds, including avocets, mallards, and herons which reproduce in the cork-oak groves on the edge of the marsh.*

The Immense
Riches of the Sea

118 *White-washed houses like these on the Balearic Islands reflect the heat of the sun and help keep occupants cooler inside.*

119 *The coast of the Balearic Islands is rather uneven and consists of a series of beaches, delightful coves, creeks, and natural ports.*

120-121 *The Island of Cabrera, situated off the southern coast of Majorca, offers the visitor transparent bays and one sandy beach on the eastern side. On the western side are the remains of a castle dating from the 14th century which functioned as a refuge for pirates during their incursions on Majorca.*

The coast of Galicia to the north of La Coruña has a lot of bays and peninsulas. A particularly panoramic one is Punta Frouxeira, near Valdoviño.

Fragments of Africa: The Canary Islands

The archipelago of the Canaries consists of seven main islands and numerous other small ones. It is situated off the western coast of Africa, and for this reason enjoys a pleasant subtropical climate. Although inhabited by a people of european stock, the Canaries have a typically African landscape with deserts and cacti in the south and fertile volcanic land in the north covered with forests and palm groves. World famous for the exportation of tropical fruits, these islands are now considered one of the paradises of European tourism, and tourism is one of the main sources of income.

124 top The clay cone of the Red Mountain, also known as "La Geria," stands out in the mysterious lunar landscape of Lanzarote.

124 bottom The Pico de Tiede, an extinct volcano, dominates the island of Tenerife. At a height of 3178 metres, it is Spain's highest mountain.

124-125 Thanks to its dark, fertile volcanic soil, the Island of Lanzarote produces and exports large quantities of vegetables and tropical fruit.

126-127 Near Maspalomas on the island of Gran Canaria, a surreal expanse of sandy dunes stretches down to the sea, creating spectacular contrasts.